An Intercessor's Pain

Dr. Kimberly K. Clayton

Written Words Publishing LLC
14189 E Dickinson Drive, Unit F
Aurora, CO 80014
www.writtenwordspublishing.com

An Intercessor's Pain © 2022 by Dr. Kimberly K. Clayton.

All rights reserved. No part of this publication may be reproduced, stored in a retrieval system, or transmitted in any form by any means, electronic, mechanical, photocopying, recording, or otherwise, without the prior permission of the author.

Published by Written Words Publishing LLC December 1, 2022

ISBN: 978-1-7356856-9-4 (paperback)
ISBN: 979-8-9873088-0-6 (eBook)

Library of Congress Control Number: 2022921085

Cover designed by Written Words Publishing LLC

Manufactured and printed in the United States of America

All Scripture quotations, unless otherwise indicated, are taken from the New King James Version. Copyright © 1979, 1980, 1982 by Thomas Nelson, Inc. Used by permission. All rights reserved. Scripture quotations noted as KJV are taken from the King James Version of the Bible, public domain. Scripture quotations noted as NIV are taken from the Holy Bible, New International Version® NIV®. Copyright © 1973, 1978, 1984, 2011 by the International Bible Society. Used by permission of Zondervan Publishing House. All rights reserved worldwide.

Dr. Kimberly K. Clayton's Books:

Available at writtenwordspublishing.com/kimberly-clayton and anywhere books are sold:

It's Praying Time: What You Need to Know About Prayer Intercession

An Intercessor's Pain

Available at Amazon.com:

It's Praying Time & Soul Winning Time

It's Praying Time & Humility Is Required

It's Praying Time & No More Idols

It's Praying Time & Obedience Is Required

DEDICATION

I would like to dedicate this book to my daughter, Elise, who has been on this spiritual journey with me, even when she wanted to do other things! Elise, you sacrificed. I see it, but most importantly, God sees it too! Mommy thanks God for you and I know I am blessed that I could be trusted with a daughter like yourself! I may not have thought to ask God for His very best concerning you, but I sure thank God that I can be trusted with His very best!

I also dedicate this book to my grandmothers, Willene, Gracie and my bonus grandmother (Great Aunt) Mary. I have been extremely blessed to have praying grandmothers like you, that pray and intercede for me and love me the way that you do!

ACKNOWLEDGMENTS

I would like to acknowledge God the Father, God the Son (Jesus Christ) and The Holy Spirit for their unconditional love and patience with me. I am forever grateful for all that God has done for me. Thank You for bringing the right people at the right time into my life! God, I see you working in my life and I thank You for never giving up on me.

I am thankful for my earthly dad, Mr. Jones, who would encourage me not to give up and to keep going even when I was hard hit by circumstances in life.

To those of you who are apart of *It's Praying Time*, I thank you for your faithfulness to pray with and for me and Elise. You too have become a part of our spiritual journey and I honor you for that!

Lastly, to every Godly Intercessor who is still on their Wall of Prayer and maintains their Prayer Watch without fail! May you be encouraged and strengthened for the journey ahead and know that I salute you!

Table of Contents

Introduction 1
Chapter 1 Not Like This! 3
Chapter 2 In Covenant with Father God 8
Chapter 3 Job the Intercessor 15
Chapter 4 I Don't Deserve This 19
Chapter 5 Jeremiah the Weeping Prophet 23
Chapter 6 A Time to Cry 27
Chapter 7 Momma, Thanks for Passing the Baton 31
Chapter 8 Tormented Like Hannah 35
Chapter 9 The Anguish of My Soul 40
Chapter 10 Judgment & Punishment 45
Chapter 11 Spiritual Depression, Darkness, Heaviness 50
Author's Biography 55

INTRODUCTION

The times we live in have presented many challenges and difficulties. Sometimes, we have to admit that even intercessors face many adversities and shed many tears in their labor of love. I invite you to go on this journey with me to see what I have faced in my faith walk and when standing in the gap for others. It's my prayer that this book encourages you and motivates you to carry on with your prayer life and your call to intercede for others. Remember, PRAY UNTIL SOMETHING HAPPENS AND IT'S PRAYING TIME!

Let's make the most of every opportunity to win souls for Jesus Christ. The truth is eternity is closer for some than others. People are leaving this world at an accelerated rate and unfortunately people are leaving this earth in very tragic ways as well. We are not just living for this life, but we are surely living for the life to come. Let me encourage you to not delay in saying this Salvation Prayer. Please repeat this prayer from a sincere heart:

Dear Lord Jesus, I know that I am a sinner and I ask You for Your forgiveness. I believe You died for my sins and rose from the dead. I turn from my sins and invite You to come into my heart and life. I ask for the Holy Spirit to dwell in me, to guide me, and to teach me all things. I choose to trust and follow You as the Son of God and Lord and Savior. In Jesus' Name. Amen and Amen!

If you repeated that prayer with a true sincerity, you JUST GOT SAVED!!! I encourage you to read your Bible on a daily basis. You can download the Bible App at https:/www.youversion.com/the-bible-app/. It will bless you greatly to be able to take the Bible with you everywhere you go. It even allows you to download offline versions of the Bible so you can read it without internet access. This Bible App also reads the Bible to you, has devotionals, Bible study plans, etc. It's the first App on my smartphone! To help you understand the scripture, please get a paper parallel study Bible that has both the King James Version (KJV) and New Living Translation (NLT) or another version of your choice.

    I am praying with you because getting saved is just the first step. Reading the Bible every day is the second step and the third step is to pray and ask God the Father to lead you to a church home where you will be planted, rooted and established in the Word of God. Be sure to find a good church home that teaches and preaches the Bible without watering it down. Many churches are still working for the Lord even if the doors of the church building are not physically open yet.

    Lastly, if you repeated the Salvation Prayer and got saved, please email me at itsprayingtime2020@gmail.com so I can pray for you and encourage you along your spiritual journey. You can also email your prayer requests and I would be glad to stand in the gap for you.

Chapter 1

NOT LIKE THIS!

There are times in life, as I pray, when I don't understand why the prayer was not answered in the way I thought, prayed and believed God for. There is an agony when I don't get the results I prayed and fasted for. Tears were shed when I prayed and gave it my all but my loved one passed away. It felt like the wind was knocked out of me, the next breath was like an eternity. How could this be? I got down on my knees and prayed with faith, boldness and urgency. I sought God for a miracle, yet it seemed that day would never come. As I grasped and clutched my chest, saying, "Lord, have mercy on me. Please don't let this be so," my heart broke and ached. How will I recover? How will I go on? Learning to love God in the bad times is a challenge I must embrace, for how can I stand in His presence with any hate? Is my heart filled with too much compassion? Oh, how I cry out, "NOT LIKE THIS!"

"Gone too soon" is what I say when I see innocent babies, children, teenagers, and young adults leaving this world in such tragic and senseless ways. We live in times when we need Almighty God to remember our children. If ever there was a time to turn back to the Lord, now is that time. I pray that we return to Father God with repented and sincere hearts for straying from Him, for repeated disobedience, for relentless pride and rebellion in our actions, words, and unfortunately in our hearts that are so far from Him. Why do our children have to suffer in such painful and tragic ways?

Someone once said to me, "When you see how bad it is getting in this world, aren't you glad they are in a better place?"

I replied, "I'm glad they are in a better place, however, I am not okay with the way they are leaving this world!"

I understand that we have to die to enter into Heaven, yet I ask the Lord, why do people have to die in such heart wrenching ways? I cry out for dignity in death. Am I wrong to want peaceful deaths for people, especially those who are most vulnerable? How do we grapple with these untimely, tragic and senseless deaths? Afterall, the way people leave here impacts you and me. Will we continue to pray and stand up for what's right? Or will our hearts become hardened, bitter and cold even though what we are experiencing has already been foretold?

As an intercessor, I am charged with keeping the faith, to pray without ceasing, to thwart the plans of the enemy. Yet the pain I'm experiencing makes my heart heavy as I fall to my knees in prayer. I sow it in tears because there are no words in this language that can fully express the sorrow I feel right down to my soul. I keep the faith because although my heart is broken and my spirit is contrite, I serve the **one and only God** who can make me **whole**. How am I able to carry on with so much hurt, pain and sorrow?

I remind myself there is hope for today and tomorrow because, **Jesus lives;** therefore, I must keep living! Because Jesus is a man acquainted with sorrows. A High Priest who is familiar with all of my pains. I gain strength and comfort in knowing that Jesus promised me He would be with me even until the very end. Jesus asked His disciples when the Son of Man returns will He find faith on Earth? I had to stop and take time to ask myself why would Jesus ask this question? Yet Matthew 24:8 is surely an answer to this question and so is 2 Timothy 3.

Life has changed so much as we know it, yet it is clear we live in the last of the last and evil days. Who would be able to stand, especially without the power of the Holy Ghost? It's clear the furnace of suffering has been turned up and it will take faith to endure until the end. I'm reminded that my faith walk is not a sprint, but a marathon that requires spiritual, physical and emotional stamina to think with the end in mind, that through

Christ Jesus victory is mine! My fortified faith is not based on my circumstance, bank accounts, achievements, or events that happen in this world. My fortified faith is based on God Almighty alone and His Holy Words, who He is and what He says. I can take it to the bank and cash the check.

Dr. Kimberly K. Clayton

Write thoughts, scriptures and prayers that come to mind below:

An Intercessor's Pain

Write thoughts, scriptures and prayers that come to mind below:

Chapter 2

IN COVENANT WITH FATHER GOD

I can't help but think that maybe if I prayed longer, harder and stronger, the results would be better. I would celebrate the victory of answered prayer, not weep in heart wrenching despair. I whisper, "I just don't understand." I'm not asking anyone to fix my pain. This is a journey I have to walk by faith and not by sight. When I hurt like this, truth be told, there's not much anyone can say that will erase my pain or bring me the victory I long for so deeply. The Lord and I are on this journey. He is the comforter I need at this very moment. Sweet Jesus, how do I go on from here? Even though I bowed low and surrendered to God, what I knew did not go as planned. Will I continue to trust in God's unchanging and faithful hand?

That remains to be seen, that even in my grief, sorrow and heavy heart, I know the God that can ease my pain and bless me with a better tomorrow. I trust Abba Father to mend my broken heart and catch every tear I shed because our covenant is real. Our intimate relationship is real. We love each other through thick and thin, the good, the bad, in sickness and health, for richer or poorer. The bond we share cannot be broken, that's how we are wed with unconditional love in the best of times and times of despair. How would we know the depths of our love for each other if it were based on the good times only? When we love each other in the tough and bad times, that's substance, depth and not phony.

Our relationship grows stronger because there is no way out of this covenant relationship. We are betrothed to one another. It's give and take in this relationship. As I grow, I learn to take the bad even when it is unfair, even when I don't understand, even when the pain runs deep, even when the tears flow and seem they won't stop, and even when it feels like my heart has bottomed out. I know my God will heal me beyond a shadow of a doubt. Father God will bless me with the strength I need to carry on. These pains and sorrows are not to break me but to cause me to bend and bow down low in the presence of Almighty God who has the power to take all my pain and transform it for His and my gain. Our partnership was never based on everything going my way. He promised me He would always be there, even until the very end. That He wouldn't forget me, He wouldn't leave me and my daily needs would be met. I know this pain won't last always. I trust God to ease my pain, mend my broken heart and strengthen me for the journey ahead.

I pray the Lord will help me to see He's working behind the scenes, healing me, and preparing me for the next assignment. Although the pain is too fresh, He promised me that even this will work for my good. OH GOD, He will help me to know that even when it doesn't look good, sound good or feel good, it is all working for my good according to Romans 8:28. There is a pain that runs deep and seems like it won't end, but I must remember that, even in this journey, with God, I won't break but I must bend. This agony, frustration and pain will come to an end...but I am reassured that Father God is with me from beginning to the end! I couldn't always see my way clearly, but His hand held my hand tight, and gave me strength when I had no might. *"He gives power to the weak, And to those who have no might He increases strength"* (Isaiah 40:29 NKJV). My tears and heartache are not in vain. They show the depths of my soul and the unwavering faith I have as I pray and believe it's already done.

I know God is real. I've seen the battles He's won. Nothing compares to the great battle-ax who fights with those who fight against me, who contends with those who contend against me. *"You are My battle-ax and weapons of war..."* (Jeremiah 51:20 NJKV). *"Contend, Lord, with those who contend with me; fight against those who fight against me"* (Psalm 35:1 NIV). As I walk through the valley of the shadow of death, I will fear no evil because Abba Father is with me (Psalm 23).

Oh, the pain I felt as those I loved and knew well passed away, yet I didn't grieve without hope. I will see them again because they died in Christ, and they will rise in Christ's eternal life too. *"But I do not want you to be ignorant, brethren, concerning those who have fallen asleep, lest you sorrow as others who have no hope"* (1 Thessalonians 4:13 NKJV). Am I selfish to want more time? Could I ever say enough to make sure they knew my love for them was real? Did I put enough quality time in with them that showed my love was sincere? Why is it that the thought of doing more for them surfaced once they passed away? Even when they told me, "Don't spend money on me, I don't need anything," my heart desired yet to do more! That's why it is so important to make it count with people while they are alive, give them their flowers while they can smell them. Even when I didn't know them, my heart wept for their passing, I had great faith they would live…this is not the outcome I prayed for…I was looking for a miracle and so much more.

Did Jesus not weep when He saw Mary and the Jews crying with heartbroken grief when Lazarus died? *"Jesus wept"* (John 11:35 KJV). Again, I must challenge myself. Why did I think this journey would be without tears, pain and intense suffering? Even in Jesus' pain, He showed love, compassion and raised the dead. So, as I follow His example, I will do the same. Jesus is calling me higher and I pray He will help me to stay focused on that to come apart and be in His presence. With all the busyness life can bring, I pray He will help me to keep Him first in all things. That I am committed to the call of intercession, in the good and bad times, especially when the words don't flow like they used to. My tears, my pressing in, my moans and groans, and my divine utterances show my sincerity and dedication to show up to travail even when it seems the battle is lost. I did as instructed and prayed and did not give up. Even when I don't know what to pray, I can count on the Holy Spirit to intercede on my behalf. *"Likewise the Spirit also helps in our weaknesses. For we do not know what we should pray for as we ought, but the Spirit Himself makes intercession for us with groanings which cannot be uttered"* (Romans 8:26 NKVJ).

On this journey of intercession, the Lord has taught me the benefits of being faithful and consistent. As I am faithful to show up to pray, intercede and cry out, I can count on Almighty God to do the rest. He taught me when I do the best then He will give me a peace and rest to carry on. The battles I face can't always be summed up as wins and losses, but my obedience, faithfulness, consistency, and humility are far more valuable as I grow in my faith walk and call to prayer intercession. God's patience with me shows as He lovingly reminds me not to give up, to keep serving Him, and to keep praying. He asked me, "Can I have a little more time with you?" Abba Father desires that intimate time with me. I pray that He teaches me to desire that quality time too. That no matter what goes on in my life, I'm determined to give Him quality time day in and day out. No longer will I blend the quality time and prayer intercession time. I cherish the time when I can just sit at my Father's feet and listen for His soft, gentle and loving words. A time when He can comfort me even when it seems the pain won't end. I feel His loving arms wrap around me so I know beyond the shadow of a doubt I can face the day and all that it brings. A time where I can receive God's divine instructions, strategies and insights on what He needs me to do.

Determined on this leg of the journey that I won't get ahead of Almighty God (like so many others in Biblical times), I do not want to go anywhere without Father God. His leading is crucial and of utmost importance to me. I like how when my heart is heavy, that I can come simply in His presence and cast all my cares knowing when the conversation and fellowship is done, I have left my burdens there. *"casting all your care upon Him, for He cares for you"* (1 Peter 5:7 NKJV).

Jesus has been a constant friend to me. I thank Him for His patience with me as I grow to be a better friend to Him. I never have to worry that He will mishandle my heart or my pain. I can count on Jesus time and time again. I realize that what I've been looking for in others is really what I found in Him. *"No longer do I call you servants, for a servant does not know what his master is doing; but I have called you friends, for all things that I heard from My Father I have made known to you"* (John 15:15 NKJV). Jesus is the best friend, the best confidant I have ever had! I value our friendship even more. I know I could never repay Him or work hard enough to earn my salvation, so by faith I am determined to be a better friend to Jesus than I have in the past.

When I feel overwhelmed, all I have to remember is that Lord Jesus is with me and Philippians 4:13 rings true in my life—**I can do all things through Christ Jesus who strengthens me**. This journey was never a solo design. It was always me and Jesus, even before time. So, since this journey is predestined, I don't have to fret. I can count on Jesus. Even when it looks like all is lost, it's not. This journey and Jesus have shown me that even when it seems at its worse, I cannot give up. I must hold on to this pain no matter how tremendous it may be. I will serve God's glorious purpose! I'm reminded that I cannot expect such glorious gain with little to no major pain. I pray the Lord forgives my unrealistic expectations as I choose to accept my reality and prepare for my destiny. I would rather face these last of the last and evil days with Jesus as my friend, confidant and Savior than without Him. I'm reminded that weeping may endure for night, but joy is coming in the morning (Psalm 30:5). So, no matter the season I find myself in, I am reassured that the valley season doesn't last always.

Write thoughts, scriptures and prayers that come to mind below:

Dr. Kimberly K. Clayton

Write thoughts, scriptures and prayers that come to mind below:

Chapter 3

JOB THE INTERCESSOR

Job was quite the intercessor. As I grow in my faith walk and intercession call, I too am learning to say, *"Though he slay me, yet will I trust in him: but I will maintain mine own ways before him"* (Job 13:15 KJV). I like that Job knew he owed no explanation to his friends, that he would take his case/plea to the judge of it all. That even though Job was suffering tremendously, he still trusted God! His relationship and faith was surely deeper than how rich and successful he was. *"But he said to her, 'You speak as one of the foolish women speaks. Shall we indeed accept good from God, and shall we not accept adversity?' In all this Job did not sin with his lips"* (Job 2:10 NKJV). Job learned how to take the good and bad in his relationship with God and remain sinless before God. I'm learning to accept the bad, but I couldn't do it without a solid prayer life.

I thank God for Job's example of a solid and mature relationship with God, that was not based on just how God had blessed him. It wasn't about the material possessions…it was about him and God. As a little girl, I would say, "Alright God, it's you and me." I still say this today. I love how God can be trusted with all of me—my good, my bad, my flaws. I'm learning not to withhold any of me from Him. Afterall, He created me. He knows me better than I know my own self. So, if the God I love and serve knows He can trust me with certain levels of pain and suffering, then I am encouraged that all of this is working for my good.

I'm a work in progress and I'm learning to work with God and not frustrate the plans He has for me. It's better when I partner with God for my breakthrough, for my process, for my deliverance instead of resisting and only delaying the fiery process even more. Job passed his test to the point that God would only hear his prayer concerning his friends that had not spoken well or true of Job or God! *"And so it was, after the Lord had spoken these words to Job, that the Lord said to Eliphaz the Temanite, 'My wrath is aroused against you and your two friends, for you have not spoken of Me what is right, as My servant Job has. Now therefore, take for yourselves seven bulls and seven rams, go to My servant Job, and offer up for yourselves a burnt offering; and My servant Job shall pray for you. For I will accept him, lest I deal with you according to your folly; because you have not spoken of Me what is right, as My servant Job has'"* (Job 42:7-8 NKJV). It's amazing how God can utilize you to pray and intercede for those who have not only wronged you, but wronged God too!

Job's story encourages me that the worst of trials don't last forever and there's a great blessing on the other side. The God I love and serve is faithful and whenever I have gone through great trials, God always rewarded me with a great blessing. I came out better than I did before. When I am tempted to throw in the towel, I know that's not an option, no way, no how! As I endure hardship like a good soldier of Jesus Christ, I continue to be a blessing. I continue to keep on pressing because I can't stay in this place of pain. Almighty God has more for me to do, so I can't focus on the pain too long because it will stagnate my process and I just can't afford to fall behind in this season. *"You therefore must **endure hardship** as a good soldier of Jesus Christ"* (2 Timothy 2:3 NKJV).

So, I've learned how to offer my broken heart, tears and pain as an additional offering to add a higher level of sincerity to the prayer and intercession, because I haven't suffered at this level not to overcome, conquer, attain, and maintain for God's glory! As I pray and intercede, it is crystal clear there can be no glory without a significant story!

Write thoughts, scriptures and prayers that come to mind below:

Dr. Kimberly K. Clayton

Write thoughts, scriptures and prayers that come to mind below:

Chapter 4

I Don't Deserve This

When I am tempted to say, "I don't deserve this," I need the Lord to help me to remember to shift to this question: "Lord, what do you want me to learn from this experience?" What insight, revelation and knowledge does God have for me to gain? All of this can't be happening for it to be in vain. What lesson am I to learn from this, that I won't forget, that can help someone else overcome when it's their turn to journey this way? Am I learning about God's sovereignty and what it really means for God to have the final say? Am I learning how to keep the faith even when the prayer wasn't answered the way I thought it should be? Is God teaching me persistence, not to waiver or buckle in my faith? How do I process the pain of what feels like unanswered prayer?

I need the Holy Spirit, the Great Comforter more than ever when the pain is intense and deeply unfair, and at times when it seems too great a burden for me to bear. The stress of a loved one dying has been a lot on me. I'm not prepared to live without my loved one. I need my loved one. How will I go on without them?

The strength to recover is what I need now, because there is more praying to do and standing in the gap especially for those who don't know how. It's these times that I must remember my faith must kick in even more, like the three Hebrew boys who knew the power of their God but would not bow down to the golden statue. It's hard to accept those things we cannot change. *"Shadrach, Meshach, and Abed-Nego answered and said to the king, 'O Nebuchadnezzar, we have no need to answer you in this matter. If that is the case, our God whom we serve is able to deliver us from the burning fiery furnace, and He will deliver us from your hand, O king. But if not, let it be known to you, O king, that we do not serve your gods, nor will we worship the gold image which you have set up'"* (Daniel 3:16-18 NKJV).

An Intercessor's Pain

Write thoughts, scriptures and prayers that come to mind below:

Dr. Kimberly K. Clayton

Write thoughts, scriptures and prayers that come to mind below:

Chapter 5

JEREMIAH THE WEEPING PROPHET

Is this why Jeremiah wept? To see what God had built through His people come burning down and His people taken into captivity could not be easy. Why weren't God's warnings heeded? Why didn't the people humble themselves right away? The pain he must have felt to see such destruction, chaos and even death. The pain had to be so deepened within, to know this anguish would be here to stay for some years and seem not to end. Bondage for God's chosen people just doesn't seem right. Didn't Jeremiah do what was right? How come he had to suffer when he walked uprightly? Why do the few have to suffer for the majority? There's got to be another way for this punishment to play out. The innocent have to cry too. If only more of God's chosen people understood how their actions and disobedience impacts the whole world; that all for one and one for all is still in effect. Then who would dare neglect God's commandments and warnings knowing the disastrous outcome? Oh, to learn from the mistakes of the past, that's the wisdom that truly lasts. Jeremiah was called, "The Weeping Prophet." Oh, how he must have cried and lamented from his soul. I pray for Almighty God to have mercy on His people, His Holy Temple and Holy Land, and give just one more warning so destruction can be avoided and punishment is no longer a part of the plan.

Oh, how Jeremiah's heart had to ache and almost literally break to see full out destruction overtake what took time to build and cultivate. The Ten Commandments and all other instructions from God's mouth must be carried to the fullest, day in and day out. Not when it is convenient, not when it is good times but in bad times too. Obeying God's commandments and warnings must be done through and through. See, Jeremiah wasn't crying wolf or playing games. He was God's genuine mouthpiece and when he said, "Thus says the Lord," it was an authentic warning from the Most High God! Even when it seems his intercession was in vain, it is clear that Jeremiah the Weeping Prophet was not to blame. Life is full of choices. God grants us free will because His commandments are not to harm us but to protect us and bless us. Yet, the opposite is true when we disobey. There are serious consequences where we are punished and endure hardships that were never intended for us. Jeremiah wept and the intercessors of today will weep too. It comes with the times and the season we live in, for no one will escape heartache.

"And you shall remember that the Lord your God led you all the way these forty years in the wilderness, to humble you and test you, to know what was in your heart, whether you would keep His commandments or not. So He humbled you, allowed you to hunger, and fed you with manna which you did not know nor did your fathers know, that He might make you know that man shall not live by bread alone; but man lives by every word that proceeds from the mouth of the Lord. Your garments did not wear out on you, nor did your foot swell these forty years. You should know in your heart that as a man chastens his son, so the Lord your God chastens you" (Deuteronomy 8:2-5 NKJV).

"I would comfort myself in sorrow; My heart is faint in me. Listen! The voice, The cry of the daughter of my people From a far country: 'Is not the Lord in Zion? Is not her King in her?' 'Why have they provoked Me to anger With their carved images—With foreign idols?' 'The harvest is past, The summer is ended, And we are not saved!' For the hurt of the daughter of my people I am hurt. I am mourning; Astonishment has taken hold of me. Is there no balm in Gilead, Is there no physician there? Why then is there no recovery For the health of the daughter of my people?" (Jeremiah 8:18-22 NKJV).

Write thoughts, scriptures and prayers that come to mind below:

Dr. Kimberly K. Clayton

Write thoughts, scriptures and prayers that come to mind below:

Chapter 6

A TIME TO CRY

The Book of Ecclesiastes mentioned that there is a time for everything including a time to cry. Oh, how that season is upon us, to see what is happening in the earth realm…how can one bear it? How can one not cry during this season? When I prayed with all my might and yet the outcome was not what was expected, my heart was heavy. Why is it pain that I gained? This season of crying and weeping doesn't seem to end. Is it because it is indeed the beginning of sorrows that Jesus foretold us about in Matthew 24:8? He warned us ahead of time what was to come. Oh, the sorrows, grief, pain and agony of back-to-back hits. It's clear that time is winding up and the closer we get to the end, the birth pains intensify. Therefore, as an intercessor, I must intensify too. All intercessors are needed to stand in the gap to fight back even when it seems the battle is being lost.

"To everything there is a season, A time for every purpose under heaven: A time to be born, And a time to die; A time to plant, And a time to pluck what is planted; A time to kill, And a time to heal; A time to break down, And a time to build up; A time to weep, And a time to laugh; A time to mourn, And a time to dance; A time to cast away stones, And a time to gather stones; A time to embrace, And a time to refrain from embracing; A time to gain, And a time to lose; A time to keep, And a time to throw away; A time to tear, And a time to sew; A time to keep silence, And a time to speak; A time to love, And a time to hate; A time of war, And a time of peace" (Ecclesiastes 3:1-8 NKJV).

We don't want to see the cost of no one praying, no one interceding. This journey we are on was never promised to be easy. When we are hardest hit, that's when our faith must kick in and we persist despite the challenges and odds that are against us. Jesus promised us He would never leave us or forsake us. Even Jesus wept, so I know, as a person and intercessor, I will too.

Let me follow the pattern that Jesus showed me to keep the faith, not to be stuck in finger pointing and blaming too, but to exercise my God given authority, power and anointing to do what Jesus did and even greater works too! *"Most assuredly, I say to you, he who believes in Me, the works that I do he will do also; and greater works than these he will do, because I go to My Father"* (John 14:12 NKJV). Jesus did not promise me a pain free, tear free ride, so when all the heartache and tears have dried, I won't abandon my faith. I have invested too much to walk away now. I am reassured of God's promises that I will be comforted now. These valley moments won't last always but these low points remind me how dependent I am on Father God and that I must keep a child-like faith to enter in. Too many mountaintop experiences would not prepare me for what's ahead. It's in the valley that I'm trained to fight, endure, trust, and keep the faith. How would I know how far I have come or not if the valley didn't appear in my life from time to time. *"Teaching them to observe all things whatsoever I have commanded you: and, lo, I am with you always, even unto the end of the world. Amen"* (Matthew 28:20 KJV).

As a servant and an intercessor, I'm called to role model a **relentless faith** and **prayer intercession** that knows **no end**. It's my faithful endurance that speaks volumes to God and to other believers and non-believers too, regardless if I lose or win. That I didn't waiver in my faith, but I persisted, and the enemy was resisted.

An Intercessor's Pain

Write thoughts, scriptures and prayers that come to mind below:

Write thoughts, scriptures and prayers that come to mind below:

Chapter 7

MOMMA, THANKS FOR PASSING THE BATON

The baton was passed to me from my mother. I had no way of knowing how intense the weight of the mantle would be. Oh, what great responsibility and pressure it is to be one of God's intercessors and friend. It's one thing to observe and watch from the outside. It's another whole level to labor and work for the Lord from the inside; where accountability, responsibility and spiritual maturity are continually enhanced from the inside out. My mother made it look so easy. Now I know her labor of love and sacrifice in prayer intercession was anything but easy. Even when she helped those who betrayed, misused and talked about her, she remained faithful to her prayer intercession. I saw her selflessness, helping and praying for others even when she needed prayer for herself.

How my mother would steal away to Jesus in hours of prayer; I know now how hard life was for her. Prayer gave her the strength to carry on. She led by example, not by mere words only but by intentional action that we saw in her daily. I can remember when things seemed held up for me, she would encourage me to ask God what He required of me. What else did I need to do before I was released from the assignment? To be patient and to keep praying, she encouraged me to never give up.

My mother's example of intercession I value the most! A praying mother is priceless. She was a rare jewel to me. Oh, how I long to hear her pray for me. This world got colder when she departed, but through steadfast prayer intercession I learned to stand and maintain my faith in Christ Jesus as my continual confession, again not just in what I say, but the lifestyle that honors ABBA Father. That is the greatest blessing!

Determined to honor her through all these life lessons learned, I didn't go through all of that for nothing…I will go higher for Jesus Christ. He allowed me to walk through the fiery furnace and yet I don't smell like smoke, and I wasn't burned. I wouldn't be who I am if my mother had not been faithful with her prayer life.

Again, a praying momma stands far above the rest, because her prayers still matter and help me to carry on. I thank my mother for always believing in me. She could see what I could not see in myself. With her, there was no giving up! I learned how to P.U.S.H. (PRAY UNTIL SOMETHING HAPPENS) through watching her. I am blessed to have had a praying mother like her, and I intend to honor her legacy by keeping the faith and holding fast to what she taught me. My mother's living legacy lives on in me and my family too.

"But they that wait upon the Lord shall renew their strength; they shall mount up with wings as eagles; they shall run, and not be weary; and they shall walk, and not faint" (Isaiah 40:31 KJV).

An Intercessor's Pain

Write thoughts, scriptures and prayers that come to mind below:

Dr. Kimberly K. Clayton

Write thoughts, scriptures and prayers that come to mind below:

Chapter 8

TORMENTED LIKE HANNAH

Sometimes, I feel pain from being tormented by certain goals, dreams and desires I had for my life. Sometimes, it seems like time is running out and it appears to be passing me by. When different women call me or pull up as they are driving by to announce they are getting married or having a baby, I am happy for them, but it seems some dreams are deferred, no matter how much I cry, "What about me?"

I can relate to Hannah in the Bible as she was tormented by her rival. She was not overcome by the torment to the point that she could not function, but she took all that torment and pain to God Almighty in prayer. Hannah prayed up out of herself until she appeared to be drunk with wine, yet she was drunk in the Lord and her fervent prayers would not be denied. God was so faithful to bless her with a son and she gave him back to the Lord as she promised and was blessed with even more children for keeping her vow to the Lord.

"Then Elkanah her husband said to her, 'Hannah, why do you weep? Why do you not eat? And why is your heart grieved? Am I not better to you than ten sons?' So Hannah arose after they had finished eating and drinking in Shiloh. Now Eli the priest was sitting on the seat by the doorpost of the tabernacle of the Lord. And she was in bitterness of soul, and prayed to the Lord and wept in anguish. Then she made a vow and said, 'O Lord of hosts, if You will indeed look on the affliction of Your maidservant and remember me, and not forget Your maidservant, but will give Your maidservant a male child, then I will give him to the Lord all the days of his life, and no razor

shall come upon his head.' And it happened, as she continued praying before the Lord, that Eli watched her mouth. Now Hannah spoke in her heart; only her lips moved, but her voice was not heard. Therefore Eli thought she was drunk. So Eli said to her, 'How long will you be drunk? Put your wine away from you!' But Hannah answered and said, 'No, my lord, I am a woman of sorrowful spirit. I have drunk neither wine nor intoxicating drink, but have poured out my soul before the Lord. Do not consider your maidservant a wicked woman, for out of the abundance of my complaint and grief I have spoken until now.' Then Eli answered and said, 'Go in peace, and the God of Israel grant your petition which you have asked of Him.' And she said, 'Let your maidservant find favor in your sight.' So the woman went her way and ate, and her face was no longer sad" (1 Samuel 1:8-18 NKJV).

"Then they rose early in the morning and worshiped before the Lord, and returned and came to their house at Ramah. And Elkanah knew Hannah his wife, and the Lord remembered her. So it came to pass in the process of time that Hannah conceived and bore a son, and called his name Samuel, saying, 'Because I have asked for him from the Lord.' Now the man Elkanah and all his house went up to offer to the Lord the yearly sacrifice and his vow. But Hannah did not go up, for she said to her husband, 'Not until the child is weaned; then I will take him, that he may appear before the Lord and remain there forever.' So Elkanah her husband said to her, 'Do what seems best to you; wait until you have weaned him. Only let the Lord establish His word.' Then the woman stayed and nursed her son until she had weaned him. Now when she had weaned him, she took him up with her, with three bulls, one ephah of flour, and a skin of wine, and brought him to the house of the Lord in Shiloh. And the child was young. Then they slaughtered a bull, and brought the child to Eli. And she said, 'O my lord! As your soul lives, my lord, I am the woman who stood by you here, praying to the Lord. For this child I prayed, and the Lord has granted me my petition which I asked of Him. Therefore I also have lent him to the Lord;

as long as he lives he shall be lent to the Lord.' So they worshiped the Lord there" (1 Samuel 1:19-28 NKJV).

Sometimes, we just don't know how we hurt one another by bragging about our good news. It reminds me to be even more mindful on how I share what God has done for me. God knows how to allow those who provoke and torment us to go higher in prayer intercession than we would without them. So, the tears I cried even for myself, and dreams deferred are not in vain.

See, Father God looks at the heart and knows what really lies within, so as long as I delight myself in Him, He promised me that He would give me the desires of my heart (Psalm 37:4)! As I pray up out of myself, God is blessing me with more than I thought I could obtain. So, like Hannah, I know how to take all the torment, frustration and pain to God Almighty in prayer where my relentless faith and persistence opens doors that only God can open.

I'm in agreement with Jesus that everything that happens isn't always who sinned, but to demonstrate God's power here on earth. *"Now as Jesus passed by, He saw a man who was blind from birth. And His disciples asked Him, saying, 'Rabbi, who sinned, this man or his parents, that he was born blind?' Jesus answered, 'Neither this man nor his parents sinned, but that the works of God should be revealed in him"* (John 9:1-3 NKJV).

Miracles are still happening today, and I am glad that they are. What an honor and a privilege it is to partner with Almighty God to let this world know God is real! He's still doing miracles, signs and wonders through me and so many others who choose to believe!

Tormentors, provokers, and agitators, do what you must quickly. God will allow me to bend but you can't break my stride, for my faith and determination is not rooted in pride, it's rooted in the Chief Cornerstone, the King of Kings, the Way, the Truth and the Life, the True Prince of Peace. The one and only Jesus Christ, the one who was hung, bled and died, and rose on the third day…that's where my relentless faith resides!

Dr. Kimberly K. Clayton

Write thoughts, scriptures and prayers that come to mind below:

An Intercessor's Pain

Write thoughts, scriptures and prayers that come to mind below:

Chapter 9

THE ANGUISH OF MY SOUL

The anguish of my soul, oh yes, it's very real. Jesus suffered in the Garden of Gethsemane the heaviness of what He was facing (the beating, the unfair trial, carrying His cross while severely injured, the crucifixion). He sought God three times in earnest prayer, "Is there any other way?" Yet, on the third time, He surrendered and said, "Thy will be done." *"He went away again the second time, and prayed, saying, O my Father, if this cup may not pass away from me, except I drink it, thy will be done. And he came and found them asleep again: for their eyes were heavy. And he left them, and went away again, and prayed the third time, saying the same words"* (Matthew 26:42-44 KJV).

Jesus knows how I feel when facing great challenges, losses of loved ones, children dying prematurely, domestic violence, gun violence, drug/opioid crisis…oh it is so much for one to bear. It's not easy for the heart to see back-to-back tragedy. Oh, woe is me as I continue to cry out, "Lord, please have mercy on those who are in trouble, suffering and need deliverance and protection. Oh, that You would make a way of escape through life and safety, for I know nothing is too hard for You."

Jesus knows what it feels like to be weighed down to the point of death, so I pray He has mercy on me when attacks and tragedies come in like a flood. I too know the anguish of the severely wounded soul. How do I go on when the pain is so strong? I follow the example of Jesus Christ and pray until God strengthens me to carry on, for I am His child and Father God

An Intercessor's Pain

knows what's best for me. I trust Him to heal me even right down to my wounded soul.

"And Ahab told Jezebel all that Elijah had done, and withal how he had slain all the prophets with the sword. Then Jezebel sent a messenger unto Elijah, saying, So let the gods do to me, and more also, if I make not thy life as the life of one of them by to morrow about this time. And when he saw that, he arose, and went for his life, and came to Beersheba, which belongeth to Judah, and left his servant there. But he himself went a day's journey into the wilderness, and came and sat down under a juniper tree: and he requested for himself that he might die; and said, It is enough; now, O Lord, take away my life; for I am not better than my fathers. And as he lay and slept under a juniper tree, behold, then an angel touched him, and said unto him, Arise and eat. And he looked, and, behold, there was a cake baken on the coals, and a cruse of water at his head. And he did eat and drink, and laid him down again. And the angel of the Lord came again the second time, and touched him, and said, Arise and eat; because the journey is too great for thee. And he arose, and did eat and drink, and went in the strength of that meat forty days and forty nights unto Horeb the mount of God" (1 Kings 19:1-8 KJV). I know if God can help Elijah who wanted to eat the cake and die, surely He will answer my cries. My pleas for help won't go unnoticed, for God's faithfulness stands true through the generations before me and even now in this current time.

For my faith overcomes any and all fears! I asked the Lord to please hear my cry while He is so near. Oh, I want to serve Him despite what happens on this faith journey. Lord Jesus shall help me to keep my eyes on Him so I won't drown in my sorrows or my anguish. I can keep going if I walk by faith and not by sight. Even when I cry, my tears are not wasted. They add value and sincerity to my prayers. In those moments, I'm not on display and my heart felt cries are definitely not for show! I'm drawing closer to the Lord than ever before because there is no way I can make it without His loving embrace and comfort for my heavy heart and soul.

Just to know God is only a prayer away encourages me that I can by faith make it the rest of the way. For He is the God that gives strength to those who are weak and have no might, that teaches my hands how to war and fight, that prays and intercedes for me when I don't know what to say. My heart is continually reassured that He will make a way even when I can't see it. I still believe in His power to save me when I need Him the most. He reminds me of the Seal of Deposit that lives in me, the Holy Ghost that is the Comforter that I need when life's heartaches manifest. I know that I am not alone and because of that I can endure this fiery trial and pass this test.

I cried those tears at night for a season and God reassured me those tears were not in vain. They added value to my purpose and destiny for my life for a reason. So, when my joyous morning comes, I'll remember the strength the Lord Jesus Christ saw me through because He paid the ultimate price. So, when temptation surfaces to throw in the towel, I cast that down quickly. It's not an option, no way, no how! I've suffered too much to give up now, so I hold on tight and refuse to let go because the Power of the Holy Ghost lives inside of me, despite all I have been through **God Almighty promised me victory**!

Write thoughts, scriptures and prayers that come to mind below:

Dr. Kimberly K. Clayton

Write thoughts, scriptures and prayers that come to mind below:

_____

_____

_____

_____

_____

_____

_____

_____

_____

_____

_____

_____

_____

_____

_____

_____

_____

_____

Chapter 10

JUDGMENT & PUNISHMENT

For judgment and punishment cannot always be avoided or even delayed. As an intercessor, I remember that God's words will be fulfilled, even those words that bring chills. Abraham did all that he could to save his nephew Lot and his family from destruction. Even with sparing their lives through his faithful intercession, Sodom and Gomorrah could not be spared for they went against God time and time again. Even with Abraham's faith counted as righteousness, God was still God and executed judgment and punishment with sheer preciseness.

"Then the men said to Lot, 'Have you anyone else here? Son-in-law, your sons, your daughters, and whomever you have in the city—take them out of this place! For we will destroy this place, because the outcry against them has grown great before the face of the Lord, and the Lord has sent us to destroy it.' So Lot went out and spoke to his sons-in-law, who had married his daughters, and said, 'Get up, get out of this place; for the Lord will destroy this city!' But to his sons-in-law he seemed to be joking. When the morning dawned, the angels urged Lot to hurry, saying, 'Arise, take your wife and your two daughters who are here, lest you be consumed in the punishment of the city.' And while he lingered, the men took hold of his hand, his wife's hand, and the hands of his two daughters, the Lord being merciful to him, and they brought him out and set him outside the city. So it came to pass, when they had brought them outside, that he said, 'Escape for your life! Do not look behind you nor stay anywhere in the plain. Escape to the mountains, lest you be destroyed.' Then Lot said to them, 'Please, no, my lords! Indeed

now, your servant has found favor in your sight, and you have increased your mercy which you have shown me by saving my life; but I cannot escape to the mountains, lest some evil overtake me and I die. See now, this city is near enough to flee to, and it is a little one; please let me escape there (is it not a little one?) and my soul shall live.' And he said to him, 'See, I have favored you concerning this thing also, in that I will not overthrow this city for which you have spoken. Hurry, escape there. For I cannot do anything until you arrive there.' Therefore the name of the city was called Zoar" (Genesis 19:12-22 NKJV).

"The sun had risen upon the earth when Lot entered Zoar. Then the Lord rained brimstone and fire on Sodom and Gomorrah, from the Lord out of the heavens. So He overthrew those cities, all the plain, all the inhabitants of the cities, and what grew on the ground. But his wife looked back behind him, and she became a pillar of salt. And Abraham went early in the morning to the place where he had stood before the Lord. Then he looked toward Sodom and Gomorrah, and toward all the land of the plain; and he saw, and behold, the smoke of the land which went up like the smoke of a furnace. And it came to pass, when God destroyed the cities of the plain, that God remembered Abraham, and sent Lot out of the midst of the overthrow, when He overthrew the cities in which Lot had dwelt" (Genesis 19:23-29 NKJV).

I pray the Lord helps me to keep the faith despite the times of sorrows and pains I live in. He made it clear that those who endure to the end are the ones who are saved, they are the ones who win! *"But he who endures to the end shall be saved"* (Matthew 24:13 NKJV). So, I will continue to do my part and trust God with all that I am and all that I got, that even when I don't understand, Father God will hold me in His unchanging hand. For these times of uncertainties, stress and calamities will not get the best of me, because I serve and love the True and Living God who works all these things together for my good. So, even in my pain, I will continue to pray and interceded like I should. I desire my faithful intercession be counted as righteousness and a blessing, that I never gave up. I persisted through life's painful lessons!

Dr. Kimberly K. Clayton

Write thoughts, scriptures and prayers that come to mind below:

Write thoughts, scriptures and prayers that come to mind below:

Chapter 11

SPIRITUAL DEPRESSION, DARKNESS, HEAVINESS

Spiritual darkness or spiritual depression, is that what it is called? The heaviness that doesn't seem to lift but reminds me that it is real and does exist. I noticed it shows up when there has been major setbacks, disasters and tragedies that just can't be explained. When I can't believe what has happened, is there nothing I can do? It's hard to accept things that are beyond one's control, to watch and pray as tragedies unfold. "Not like this" is the cry that is deep within my soul!

A heart of compassion is hurting deeply. Who knew this would play out this way? Despite all of this, I will continue to pray. I've seen this spiritual darkness, depression and heaviness show up as God prepares me for the next promotion and elevation in Him. It's all a part of His process for me. As I grow in Him, I understand there are impurities in me that cannot stay, so as uncomfortable as the fiery furnace feels, it is indeed a part of the process. I have to come out standing and as pure as gold. I am reassured my journey is on the right track as the greatest of all, Jesus Christ, suffered this agony in the Garden of Gethsemane and on the cross too! Job, Elijah, Hannah, Mother Theresa, Martin Luther King Jr., and Nelson Mandela, just to name a few, all suffered through some form and level of spiritual depression too.

Amazingly, they did not let it stop them from achieving their destinies and greatness in God. I thank God for their examples and I am encouraged to fulfill my destiny and help others reach theirs too! There's a press deep within that won't allow me to stop. Even this spiritual depression can't make me give in. I understand that some assignments are far more challenging than others. Standing in the gap for those who are suicidal, homicidal, mentally ill, drug addicted—those whose lives hang in the balance. There's an extra pressure to those assignments, how could it not be?

I won't let the negativity of people who don't know what it is to carry such heavy assignments interfere with me. Since assignments like these are kept in the strictest confidence, I'll leave them to their ignorance. See, they have to walk a real long mile in my shoes to understand what it is really like to place the needs of others before your own. I'm determined to show God I can be trusted with the assignments He gives me, without defending myself and without explanation to others. **I report to God Almighty and no one else!**

Assignments like these take a great deal of investment of time, energy and effort. These intense assignments take a much stronger warfare prayer that is consistent and persistent. There's no slacking in this area, that's for sure. I have to show up, even in person, to really demonstrate that I care, to prove that the individual isn't battling suicidal thoughts, anxiety, mental illness, or addiction alone, to reinforce that I am with them until they are strong enough to stand on their own. These are the assignments that can't be abandoned, even when I'm facing my own spiritual depression and other attacks too. It's no wonder, as an intercessor, I can feel depleted and drained. This is no ordinary load that I'm carrying.

When I am tempted to complain, I remember all of those who stood in the gap for me until I had enough strength to stand. I realize how they were facing greater challenges than I ever knew about, yet I could count on them day in, day out. It's in these times, I gird myself up and ask the Lord for extra strength to carry out the assignments to completion. I will not underestimate the power of prayer. God sees my faithfulness and knows I desire that those whose lives hang in the balance live and not die declare the works of the Lord (Psalm 118:17).

Even in the heaviness of the assignment, what an honor and a privilege it is to stand with those who are facing some of the lowest points in their lives; to see them overcome the enemy of their soul is worth more than pure gold. It gives me encouragement to keep running for Jesus Christ. Even when spiritual depression seems to be so heavy on me, I'm learning to build an altar on my heart where I meet with Father God with a genuine sincerity, where I can be authentically me. When I can tell Father God all my concerns about the assignments and the heaviness I feel, I know all my wounds, pressure and depression Abba Father heals.

See here, I am not afraid to praise God in the midst of great adversity, for when my heart is heavy, He strengthens me to finish the assignments and to keep going for His glory! I am reminded that the heaviness I feel comes with the territory, so I keep praying and standing in the gap because time is winding up. *"I must work the works of Him who sent Me while it is day; the night is coming when no one can work"* (John 9:4 NKJV). It's time to redeem the time and make it count so God gets the glory out of my story!

"See then that you walk circumspectly, not as fools but as wise, redeeming the time, because the days are evil. Therefore do not be unwise, but understand what the will of the Lord is. And do not be drunk with wine, in which is dissipation; but be filled with the Spirit, speaking to one another in psalms and hymns and spiritual songs, singing and making melody in your heart to the Lord, giving thanks always for all things to God the Father in the name of our Lord Jesus Christ, submitting to one another in the fear of God" (Ephesians 5:15-21 NKJV).

Write thoughts, scriptures and prayers that come to mind below:

Write thoughts, scriptures and prayers that come to mind below:

AUTHOR'S BIOGRAPHY

Dr. Kimberly K. Clayton has her Christian Counseling Certificate, Community Chaplain License, Master's in Biblical Studies, and Honorary Doctorate in Prayer and Intercession from Ecclesia Leadership Institute (https://ecclesialeaders.info). She is currently working on another Biblical project with goals to represent Jesus Christ to the fullest, win as many souls for Jesus Christ as possible, recruit and train additional Godly intercessors, and to continue to pray and intercede as God has called her to do. She lives in the Midwest with her daughter, Elise, who is her pride and joy!

She is the leader of It's Praying Time, where prayer, intercession and training takes place on their YouTube Channel (www.youtube.com/@ItsPrayingTime). Every third Saturday, Corporate Prayer is at 10:00am CST. Dr. Kimberly believes in the power of prayer and intercession and is determined to help others grow in the area of prayer and intercession as well. It's Praying Time is focused on reaching as many souls for Jesus Christ as possible through various platforms.

Dr. Kimberly also is an Ordained and Licensed Minister through School of the Prophet led by the fearless leader, Prophetess Renee Gordon! One of her most prized moments is that herself and her daughter, Elise, had their second baptism together through School of the Prophet.

www.ingramcontent.com/pod-product-compliance
Lightning Source LLC
Chambersburg PA
CBHW070337120526
44590CB00017B/2921